THE CHAIR

THE CHAIR

Prose Poems by

Richard Garcia

South Huntington Public Library
145 Pidgeon Hill Road
Huntington Station, NY 11746

AMERICAN POETS CONTINUUM SERIES, No. 145

BOA EDITIONS, LTD. ❧ ROCHESTER, NY ❧ 2014

Copyright © 2014 by Richard Garcia
All rights reserved
Manufactured in the United States of America

First Edition
14 15 16 17 7 6 5 4 3 2 1

For information about permission to reuse any material from this book please
contact The Permissions Company at www.permissionscompany.com or e-mail
permdude@eclipse.net.

Publications by BOA Editions, Ltd.—a not-for-profit corpo-
ration under section 501 (c) (3) of the United States Internal
Revenue Code—are made possible with funds from a variety
of sources, including public funds from the New York State
Council on the Arts, a state agency; the Literature Program
of the National Endowment for the Arts; the County of Mon-
roe, NY; the Lannan Foundation for support of the Lannan
Translations Selection Series; the Mary S. Mulligan Chari-
table Trust; the Rochester Area Community Foundation; the
Arts & Cultural Council for Greater Rochester; the Steeple-
Jack Fund; the Ames-Amzalak Memorial Trust in memory of Henry Ames,
Semon Amzalak and Dan Amzalak; and contributions from many individuals
nationwide. See Colophon on page 94 for special individual acknowledgments.

ART WORKS.
arts.gov

State of the Arts

NYSCA

Cover Design: Sandy Knight
Interior Design and Composition: Richard Foerster
Manufacturing: McNaughton & Gunn
BOA Logo: Mirko

Library of Congress Cataloging-in-Publication Data

Garcia, Richard, 1941–
[Poems. Selections]
The chair : prose poems / by Richard Garcia. — First edition.
    pages cm
ISBN 978-1-938160-44-8 (paperback) — ISBN 978-1-938160-45-5 (ebook)
I. Title.
PS3557.A71122A6 2014
811'.54—dc23
                    2014004779

BOA Editions, Ltd.
250 North Goodman Street, Suite 306
Rochester, NY 14607
www.boaeditions.org
A. Poulin, Jr., Founder (1938–1996)

Contents

MATCHBOOK

My footsteps are loud, as if I were in a large room. I find a book of matches in my pocket and light one. I almost burn my fingers as the light goes out, leaving a trace of sulfur in the air. I try another and hold it high. Ropes. Curtains. I kneel, holding the match low. Wooden floor. I walk ahead slowly, sliding my feet, and almost step off into space. I hear a gasp. Someone chuckles. Apparently I'm being watched. I count the matches. I don't want to waste any. Maybe I can find a candle. A flashlight. A light switch. I prepare myself to light the next match. I'm getting better at this.

A Portrait of My Childhood Painted by Goya

In the kitchen an infant is standing in a corner as if he were shackled upright. He hears his mother calling softly, *Camínate, niñito.* Older now, he is trying to count to five. A hooded inquisitor from the Church stands over him. The boy cannot seem to get past five. The Inquisitor slaps his belt against a table: Count! The boy counts, rapidly from one to ten in English, then rapidly from ten to one in Spanish. The shadow of a wolf disappears into the wall. A slow pan of the kitchen: colander, knives, a cleaver. Voiceover: Bombs away! Geronimo! Ai Cisco! Ai Pancho! Hi-ho Silver, away! The boy opens his eyes many years later but he is still in the kitchen. His father is wrestling with a huge bird. Is it a turkey, a chicken? His father is behind the bird holding its wings out, laughing. The boy closes his eyes. Through the smoky sky, an old man clings to the back of an enormous bird.

Day at the Beach, 1958

You are on your knees in the sand, praying to Cupid. Diane is making a castle complete with stairwell. Your secret thoughts are longing for Clementine. And Lucy, remember her? You're in a circular haze. That's what you get for staring at the whirligig called Spike the Junkyard Dog. Maybe you could grab that propeller for your beanie. But lucky for you, your aviator goggles look great pushed up on your forehead. You want to tell Lucy about your collection of bongos, but she is busy smiling into her compact mirror, just for you. What a waste. What a waist Diane has—and what spindles for legs, that Clementine, but her breasts are the threshold to dreams. That *gordito* in your bathing suit makes you walk as if you were crippled when you wander off with her toward the Cave of Making Out. The cave where time chills your feet. She, demure beside you, sitting like a lady, offers tea. The teapot, tethered to balloons, floats into the sky. A teapot tethered to balloons floating into the sky. Almost famous. Like Frankie Avalon. That was the day Cupid missed but Anteros smiled. Kissing Clementine goodbye, you even said *adios* to her parents. Rode off in the back seat sitting between Lucy and Diane. Lucy asleep with her cheek against your shoulder; Diane asleep with head in your lap.

THE UNSTUCKS AT THE GATES OF THE DESERT FOLLY GARDEN

My branch of the family is unstuck-together. On the Mexican vaudeville circuit they were known as *Los Desemepegados*—The Unstucks. Back in those days there were many offshoots of the family, and they all hated each other. The Barcelona Unstucks hated the Paris Unstucks, all because of a one hundred-dollar bet that a cow would go up and down stairs. The Cyprus Unstucks hated the Jerusalem Unstucks, all because of a key that was hidden and lost. The Las Vegas Unstucks hated the Tijuana Unstucks; that feud was over who had the right to claim the invention of the Caesar salad. There were circus Unstucks, aerialists, who were known as The Flying Unstucks. They were famous for not catching each other. Every ten years the Unstucks come together, in a manner of speaking, at the Unstucks reunion.

Since the late eighteenth century, the reunion has been held at the Gates of the Desert Folly Garden. There is even a famous photo of the reunion you can get on the Web for a hundred dollars. It is mislabeled "André Breton and the Surrealists at the Gates of the Desert Folly Garden." Perhaps one of the Unstucks lied about the identity of their party to the photographer.

The Unstucks meet and register for the reunion under false names, at the statue of the giant dangling a large naked woman by the ankles. To avoid conflicts they all don masks and wear the same face the whole time. It is a bald, eyebrow-less idiot face with a blank expression. During the reunion they even sleep with the bald, eyebrow-less, idiot face with a blank expression mask on. If two Unstucks happen to become amorous, say, in the pyramid-shaped icehouse, they leave the masks on. They even make love with the masks on; that way, no Unstuck is angry or jealous during the reunion, and they can go their separate ways without knowing from which branch of the family either one hailed.

Once, a couple of strangers, perhaps an English couple, wore bald, eyebrow-less idiot face with the blank expression masks and crashed the reunion. Apparently they liked it so much that they came back every ten years for the rest of their lives. In fact, it is believed that every ten years, two of their descendants crash the reunion wearing bald, eyebrow-less idiot face with the blank expression masks. But no one knows this for sure.

Like the yo-yo and the boomerang, the first umbrellas were created as weapons. Naked warriors, their bodies painted with streaks of blood, would dance, holding their umbrellas in threatening positions. They would point them at the sky, flapping them open and closed, and stab the air with their umbrellas; however, they soon learned they could trip on their umbrellas during the confusion of battle. Or, as they charged the enemy, they would waste time trying to get their umbrellas open. Worse, as they approached the enemy holding their umbrellas like parasols, like tightrope walkers or ballerinas, the enemy would laugh at them. It was to be centuries before anyone thought of using umbrellas in the rain. Even today, umbrellas lie abandoned at airports, train stations, waiting rooms, hallways, and porticos.

The first white anklets fell from the sky during the age of the dinosaurs. Nobody knew what they were because there was nobody to wonder. Dinosaurs poked at them with their snouts, but since they had never been worn, they had no scent. One anklet hung from a branch of the first primordial tree. A volcano erupted, covering the tree with lava. The branch and the anklet became a fossil. Today, that fossil is stored in the basement of the Smithsonian. It has always puzzled scientists. What is it, that thing hanging from what could be a tree branch? One theory is that it is the ancestor of all flowers. In Victorian times poets wore white anklets to bed. The anklets were attached to each other by pearl buttons. It was thought that the anklets, buttoning their feet together, would prevent the poets from walking in their sleep. Even today, you can see white anklets of famous poets in the White Anklet Museum in the very small town of One House, Nevada. Granted, few people visit the White Anklet Museum in One House, Nevada. Few people visit One House, Nevada. But those who take the time to do so are never disappointed.

As little George Washington prepared to chop down the cherry tree, he got an idea. What if he were seen chopping down the tree? So he blackened his face with a burnt cork. Now if he were seen, it would be blamed on one of the slave children. Little George was seen that day, but only by the slave children, who thought this looked like fun. Sneaking into the kitchen, they dipped their faces and hands in flour. Back in the yard, they played at being white people. They stood tall; they spoke slowly, gave each other commands, and danced their version of a minuet. The children were seen by their parents, and by the overseers, and by little George's father. What fun, they all thought, and thus began the tradition, that one day a year the slaves would paint their faces white and become like the masters. The masters would paint their faces black and become like the slaves. They would take commands from the slaves, slap their knees, tell jokes, dance, and have a good time. And so on through history—Pat Boone became Little Richard and sang a song he thought might be about ice cream. Even across the ocean, Mick Jagger, an accounting student listening to the blues in his dorm, lost his English accent and learned to talk just like Muddy Waters. Oh Mississippi Delta, Oh Africa, Oh harp and fiddle and banjo. Oh young Elvis, visited in a dream by the ghost of his twin, Jesse. In the dream Jesse was black, whispering, *Brother, when you sing, sing like a black man, dance like a black man.* Elvis quit his job at the trucking company that day, and began to sing as no white man had sung before.

LITTLE KNOWN FACT NUMBER ONE

Perry Como had rabid animal attacks. Backstage, after a performance, he would lie on the floor of his dressing room thrashing about, foaming at the mouth. They had to tie him to a board with ropes, soft ones so they would not redden or bruise his tender skin. Sometimes, when his rabid animal attack was really bad, they would wrap him in two sheets and soak them with water. Even Houdini, who also was known to have rabid animal attacks, had a hard time escaping from wet sheets wrapped around his body. Allow me to introduce myself, I am a character from another poem. Suddenly I woke up in this one, although my presence has no bearing here. The poem I was in was an ode to bodily fluids. It went, O fluids, thou unsung thou miraculous bearers of love tidings, envelopes of DNA—but here I am lying on the floor of what appears to be a dressing room, next to a man whose head is protruding from wet sheets. He is foaming at the mouth. Perhaps that is why I am here, to observe and report on the rivulet of clear saliva sliding down his chin and onto the worn blue carpet.

Little Known Fact Number Two

Rilke was inspired to write *The Duino Elegies* while watching Jackie Gleason on *The Honeymooners*. It was his favorite show. He and Lou, his girlfriend, would sit up in bed in front of their TV.

This was at her place and her bedroom was full of dolls she had won at fairs. Rilke did not like the dolls and Lou always had to make sure all the dolls' eyes were closed when he came over. Otherwise he thought they were staring at him. Lou had been a patient of Freud's and she would try and get Rilke to talk about why he did not like the dolls. But he just sat there staring at *The Honeymooners*. He did not want to talk about the little dresses he had to wear when he was a child, or the dolls his parents gave him for Christmas, or the fact that his middle name was Maria.

The sound on their set was not so good and he did not know English anyway so he thought it was a serious show. He liked the way Art Carney would make exaggerated gestures when he was about to sign his name. He adopted that affectation when he signed his books at poetry readings.

One night Jackie Gleason raised his fist to Alice and threatened to send her to the moon. Rilke interpreted the gesture as a plea for celestial intervention. Just at that moment the eyes of a doll that was on top of the TV came open and stared, it seemed, right into his soul.

All at that same moment Art Carney came down the fire escape and climbed in the kitchen window, the doll stared at him, and the sound of their TV went out. Rilke thought of angels descending through the empty silence of the universe down a fire escape of stars. He thought of angels climbing in the window, of an angel writing something in a book with exaggerated gestures as if it were conducting a symphony.

Leonardo da Vinci, Isaac Newton, and Albert Einstein always put their left shoe on first. This occurs to you as a clerk in the shoe store brings you the right shoe of the pair you are considering. Sorry, you say, but Leonardo da Vinci, Isaac Newton, and Albert Einstein always put their left shoe on first and I always do the same. It is written that Jesus always put his left sandal on first. He also advised his disciples to put their left sandal on first. He said, Verily, if your message is not received, leave that village and shake its dust off your sandals. I assume he meant to shake the left sandal first. Putting your left shoe on first sends a message to your brain. Message to brain: Leonardo da Vinci, Isaac Newton, and Albert Einstein always put their left shoe on first. And you, whoever you are, technician, employee, wife, lover, friend, you who dress me for the last time, please, put my left shoe on first.

THE RELIGIOUS BRAIN

A man's brain would fly out of his head to attend midnight Mass. This bothered him because he was not religious. Sometimes the man wanted to use his brain after midnight, but it was attending Mass. So he would just sit there, perhaps with a remote in his hand, wondering what it was that he had wanted to do. But how could he wonder without a brain? Well, he looked like he was wondering, sitting there in front of a turned-off TV with a remote in his hand. Besides, he had read somewhere that intelligence was everywhere, that matter itself was formed of intelligence, so who needs a brain anyway? One night, the night custodian at the church mistook the man's brain for a sponge, and used it to clean up a mess in one of the pews. The brain made a good sponge. The custodian stored the brain in the closet with his other tools. The man whose brain would fly off to midnight Mass hardly missed his brain. After all, how could he know he missed his brain if he did not have a brain?

A man could not sleep. He supposed it was because he was to be executed in the morning. Bummer, he thought. He picked at his belly button. Something he seldom did. There were grains of sand in his navel. He wondered if he should have done this more often. Soon there was a pile of sand in his cell. Then sand dunes. He wandered off into the dunes.

He drank from cactus and the occasional well. He covered his head with things he found, scraps of cloth, chunks of Styrofoam. He found pieces of metal and plastic. He met others out there. Several men and one woman, rivals, were searching for artifacts left behind from the sets of *Star Wars* movies.

He could tell from the tilt of the constellations that he was walking back in time. One evening he stumbled upon the Last Supper. A Passover dinner, but there were no chairs. He inquired of one of the disciples and was told this is the custom. It is meant to show their haste in preparing to leave Egypt.

James, brother of Jesus, was holding forth. He made a joke about matzo being the world's first fast food. No one laughed. Jesus was quiet. He seemed to be in a funk. One of the disciples asked the first of the four questions: Why is this night different from all other nights?

The disciples all turned toward Jesus. Jesus said, Forget all that, let's make this night about me, no matzo, no Egypt, no Moses; henceforth, this wine shall be my blood, and this bread shall be my flesh and you shall consume it—no sacrificial lamb with unbroken legs, for I shall be the sacrifice.

The man who could not sleep wandered off, down the back stairs and into the alley. He set off for the desert in the vague direction of where his cell had been. Soon he was joined by Judas. Neither man spoke.

MY ANGRY MOB

First you see the lights of their torches bobbing in the distance. Closer, there is Miriam, the housewife and proud of it, in her polka-dot muumuu, waving a rolling pin. Clyde the blacksmith in his leather apron, waving his favorite ball-peen hammer. Farmer Blandini with his pitchfork, red-faced, his jaw clenched. Jolene, the librarian, who in her haste, drops her glasses, cracking one lens. The school nurse cradling a shotgun; the paperboy, a rake over his shoulder. Preacher Bob, with a Bible in one hand, a hatchet in the other. My angry mob out on the front lawn. Some carry rope, some bricks, rocks, staves, and skillets. My angry mob, sometimes they yell, There he is—get him! But tonight they're quiet, mumbling among themselves, milling about, kicking the grass, up to no good, sounding like the leaves of the magnolia tree rattling in the wind.

My Fog

My fog sits sulking in the corner. It only spoke twice. It said, Please. Later it said, Thank you. I don't know why or for what. I know not all fogs are so polite. What about the fog that forms on the mountain and creeps downward, full of enemy soldiers? They carry no guns or grenades, just daggers and swords. What about the killer London fog? The poisonous fog that was sleeping on the bottom of a lake until the lake turned over in its sleep? If I look at the corner where my fog sits, of course it is gone. When I look away the fog resumes its vigil. I hear a foghorn in the distance. It sounds like it is calling out, Your fog. Another foghorn answers it. My fog. Your fog. My fog. I get up and look out the window. Across the street I catch a glimpse of a house I have never seen before. Maybe it was part of a flock of houses migrating through the fog to their winter lots. Yes, that could happen. Everything is moving after all. Just like Los Angeles. One day you look up and see a mountain looming over the distance. Next day it is gone.

Helen's Birthday

One February fourteenth a cloud came to stay at Helen's house. The cloud did not know it was Valentine's Day. It did not know it was Helen's birthday. It was a shy cloud, and was hiding from the rudeness of cannon fire, although the war had been over for some years. It was the only cloud that had rained fountain pens. Helen sat on the couch with the cloud each afternoon. She told it her secrets. She whispered to the cloud, I saw Mia Farrow in her underwear. The cloud was glad it came to her house. Sometimes the cloud would leave an antique fountain pen between the cushions. It liked to look out the window at the passing clouds. Although the cloud never spoke, Helen knew the dropped pens were signs of affection. She read to the cloud stories of trying times. Often she closed her eyes and imagined she was a nightclub dancer in Cairo, Egypt, but she was really an Allied spy known to her handlers by the code name Tiffany. Helen showed the cloud her awards and diplomas. Her awards and diplomas that lined the wall above the couch. Her awards and diplomas that drifted across the wall in the morning light.

SUSAN

When Susan was four years old, she had a cirrus cloud for a pet. She named it Serious. Serious used to call her by her middle name, Laughter. They would play. Serious could become a painted turtle. Sometimes he would pretend to be smoke from the war. One day a paper machine followed her home from school. She did not know if it was a machine made of paper, or a machine that made paper. Or was it Serious, pretending to be a paper machine? In her private life, the life she lived while she was sitting at the bottom of the attic stairs, she played the violin for the ocean. The ocean would stop its waves and listen. She could play a song about doors opening and closing. On the evening before her fifth birthday, Susan threw a red handkerchief made of silk into the sky. It rose up and did not fall back to earth. It was a present for Serious: This is for you, she said, as she flung it upwards, you can use it if you cry. The next morning, when she woke, there was something clenched in her hand. Still half-asleep, lying on her side, she watched her hand opening. It was something small and white. Holding her palm up to her eyes, she saw it was a tiny feather.

CHRISTINA

When your hands pretend to pray, even the sky is convinced and supplies appropriate lighting. Sometimes your hands take you dancing. This way, your left hand might say as it pushes aside a curtain of shattered glass. No, this way, your right hand says—Here, steal these flowers from a cemetery. Now you kneel to cup a pool in your hands. You rummage through a waterfall. Now your hands drift over a forest, screeching like a pterodactyl. Small creatures hide from the shadow of your hands. But it is all the same dance, the dance of your hands leading the way. Your hands push the sun into a cloud. You pull evening toward your belly, fold it like a napkin and put it in a box. The box is in a room. The room is in your hands. No church or steeple. A bare light bulb. No furniture except for the box. You sit on the floor. Your hands nestle into your lap and go to sleep. Tonight your hands will dream about you.

Miss C.C.

A woman thought she had too many Cs in her name. She took her name and wrote it many times on many sheets of paper. On a country road she waited for the wind. The wind came. She threw the many pieces of paper in the air. Spinning her names in a circle, the wind took them to a secret place. It was a small room behind a bathtub. The woman felt free of her name. Her name with all its Cs. She walked back along the country road. She had a trick that only she could do that caused gophers to peek out of their burrows. She could observe telephone conversations inside wires that crisscrossed the night. She saw the color blue and wondered what it was used for. In the morning she woke without her name. She decided she liked Ss so she named herself See-See. She wondered if the wind that took her old name would cast a shadow. She wondered if the shadow would resemble her.

OCTOBER

Every night I have a dream. A pickup blonde. An ice-pick. I need one of those croakers you tell dreams to. Every night I have a dream. A pickup truck. A blonde. A deadly game of pickup sticks. Every night the house I grew up in. The clean sneak. The shiv. The clip-joint. Every night the showdown in the mirrored room. An ice-pick in the ear looks like a brain hemorrhage. I kill somebody. Or somebody kills me. I'm not sure. Morning hits me like a blackjack. I can't crab the dream. I'm such a daisy; my feet are rooted in the sheets. You tell your dream, you don't have to dream it anymore. If you don't believe in dreams you won't die in your sleep. Thursday, Friday, Saturday, the last slice of the moon's decapitation. Now you can put someone else's face over your own.

So many candles. A book leans against a doorway. Drunk again. Listen Bud: there is no such color as beige. The hosts, both sitting on the couch, are making up dialogue to Korean soap operas: Feel my hat . . . It is taller than your hat . . . You have stupid hat. Meanwhile the guests line up for their gifts. Lucky Strikes. Eagles Milk spread on white bread. A fishing lure. And now the latest news: the color blue has become a special kind of money. In Los Angeles, autumn now lasts fifteen minutes. They listen in disbelief. Finger bones scratch bony chins. One recalls how she admired the little sugar skulls last year. Now she has one all her own. It even has her name on its forehead. Just in from the other side of the wallpaper: same old, same old.

Former Lovers

One joins a cult and goes to India to escape you. Another becomes super-orthodox and follows a rabbi rumored to be the Messiah. It makes you wonder, what is it about you that drives women toward God? One sends you empty envelopes. Only one ever comes to see you again. She wants your advice on the nature of evil. They form covens. They make little dolls that look like you. They come to your readings and snort whenever you read a love poem. One sends you a package that contains a colorless, odorless powder. After you wake from a fitful sleep they remain in your dream and discuss it among themselves. They say you are washed up. Your poems are red sails in the sunset. They want to give you a Viking funeral while you're still alive. The one in India lives in a cave. She has become a holy woman. She sends you a bill for a set of dentures. The one who came back to see you has become a man. She wants you to change your sex and marry her. The rabbi rumored to be the Messiah is wanted for embezzlement. He escapes to Canada hiding in the trunk of your former lover's car. You remember her. Her father was a famous writer, who, peeved that you did not play tennis, challenged you to a duel. Her skin was smooth as vinyl.

FOOTSTEPS

Not tapping metallically, as one crossing a courtyard in hobnail boots, or a busker pacing in an alcove of The Plough and Thistle, not pathetic, one shoe flapping, its sole attached with twine. Not the scrape of one dragging a brass bed, but a measured, reassuring, firm-yet-soft pat of leather against pavement crunching the occasional leaf—the footsteps of one who hears the clatter of dishes and soft voices drifting out of rooms as balm and longing. While above, in the open spaces between the cypress trees, pelicans drift toward their island nests. The sun setting in the sea. Dark water. Gray sky, clouds illumined from below. One star. No, a planet.

The Masked One

He slept with a T-shirt over his face. Thus no one in his dreams recognized him. But if they did, they were discreet, referring to him only as The Masked One. Once, his large dog fell asleep in his arms in front of the television set. He thought nothing of it, but that night the sensation stayed in his arms and he dreamt he held a dying child. When he stayed at hotels in his dreams, he used an alias. He left items behind in these hotels, but he often forgot which alias and which hotel. When he held the dying child, he cried as he never had before. He woke feeling very happy. He slept with a T-shirt over his face. It rose and fell over his mouth, as if he were a covered statue come to life.

SAPPHO

If not, winter, violets in her lap, golden-sandaled dawn . . . Sappho is talking in her sleep again. She is dreaming of Egypt. She is dreaming of bandages. She says, Angels look like normal people. Together we step inside a bubble. It takes us under the Aegean Sea. It's supposed to be the backyard behind the house where I grew up. Sappho and I are third-graders home from school. We are wrestling on the grass together. She is wearing a plaid cowboy shirt. Sappho sits on my chest. Outlined against the sky, she reminds me of Dale Evans. I tell her she looks like Dale Evans. This may be my first attempt at poetry. Sappho laughs and bounces on my chest. My words are small bubbles that rise into the sky.

I was leading the poetry workshop that was famous for being like the French Revolution happening in reverse. My wit flowed like a child riding a tricycle in the calm eye of a hurricane. But the students stared at me, as if I were a slow-motion film of a murder-suicide. The light and shadows of an entire week of Venetian blinds dragged its prison bars across my face. All weapons and cash on the table, I declared. Soon the poetry workshop looked like a mobsters' poker game in the back room of a casino. We brought out the Havanas. Then we became poker-playing dogs. I was a collie. Most of the students were mutts; one, Jock, had one ear up and one down. But Basil, a poet in the epic mode, was a borzoi. He wore a monocle. We decided to pose for a photo in a tableau of famous poets. As a collie, and leader of the Poker-Playing Dog Poetry Workshop, I got to be Walt Whitman. Mo, a pug-faced chihuahua-bulldog mix, was Emily Dickinson.

Charles and I are painting a wall in my childhood room. This is how we teach a poetry lesson at Harvard. A minor official from the Dean's Office comes to see us. He can barely suppress a smirk as he tells us, in his fake British accent, that the Dean is not pleased. Our paint is peeling after it dries. The spackling is showing through under the paint; obviously, we did not prime it. And the wall was supposed to be Navajo Pink, not Boneyard White. In short, bad poetry lesson and our services are no longer required. Well, I remark, feigning indifference, I bet those Greeks forgot to prime their temples and statues too. So that's just hooplabumky. And in case you don't know what that is, Mr. Minor Functionary, that is when you feel all alone, abandoned like a country bumpkin on a basketball court, but the squeegee of indifference wipes the window of your mind clear and dry. Charles, being more experienced in academia, says nothing. We gather up our tools and climb out the window, over the fence, down the alley and into the street. It is San Francisco in the late forties. Technically, Charles hasn't been born yet. But hell, we're poets, and as the wind blows right though our bodies, we wish the wind well.

The Expert

I am an expert at dying in slow motion. I know, the giant in the barn in the movie *Seven Samurai* was thought to be the first, but I was dying in slow motion long before dying in slow motion was even invented. There are three things you need for dying in slow motion. The first is, you have to be able to find things in the dark. Even in a strange room, one you have never been in before, you have to be able to kneel in the dark and recover your companion's earring from inside her slipper, no searching, on the first try. The second is, you have to always be mistaken for someone who looks just like you. Long ago, I walked into a shop and the young lady behind the counter said, It's you! Yes, I replied, it's me. No, she said, it's really you. This went on for a while. Finally I asked her out, but she refused, because I was me. As I left, I turned back and said, Yes, it is me, and I'll never forget that night in Singapore when you gave me your answer. My God! she cried, it really is you! The third thing you need for dying in slow motion is unknown. Some say it is the ability to appear to fall slowly and to land softly.

Others say you have to long for someplace or someone that never existed. But I think if you knew what the third thing was, you would not be able to die in slow motion. You would not be able to die so slowly that those who have paid to observe you die in slow motion will be dead before your limp body touches the ground.

Useful Phrases for Business Letters: Example One

I am contacting you regarding the peek-a-boo umbrella. I assume that one should ignite a crust of apogee while setting out on a journey of such import. Disregard the peek-a-boo umbrella. Let us pursue fandango, lurid alibis, the juxtaposition of a winged heart and lettuce, or a winged hart leaping over the Van Allen belt. Nor do I refer to the pain of needles circling the planet. I mean megaphones of lucidity; I wish to draw your attention to what I'm talking about. Please find enclosed a photograph of a famous person's teeth. Memorandum: For we shall gather at the river. *Note: If you don't know the famous person's name, in conclusion you may use "Faithfully yours" or "Yours faithfully"; barring that, please return to Useful Phrases for Business Letters: Example One.*

In this age, no one thinks about the Typewriter of Transcendence. Perhaps because, unlike other typewriters, it is very quiet. The keys type themselves as it takes dictation softly, so as not to wake you. The Typewriter of Transcendence. It has all the letters of all the alphabets. It has all the characters of languages that have no alphabets. If you lift it up and slam it down in anger, there is no need to call a technician in Calcutta who is well versed in American baseball, nor a prisoner in Alabama, who will read to you from a script. In a rage after a series of dull dreams, dreams inspired by events of the day, a sound in the night, a television program, like reruns of *Mannix* for instance, you throw the Typewriter of Transcendence out the third-story window of your small apartment. You wait by the window, listening, waiting for it to explode against the pavement. But there is no sound, as if you had thrown it through a hole in the earth. Later, the Typewriter of Transcendence reappears on your desk, as if, silly boy, you had ever even considered throwing away the Typewriter of Transcendence.

The Pencil of Transubstantiation slides across the page like a figure skater dressed as an undertaker. An undertaker with an expression of fake concern. But let us praise the faults of the writer guiding the Pencil of Transubstantiation across the frozen pond of the page. Fault number one: praise to him for stealing a pumpkin pie and claiming he was bringing it to the children at the hospital. Fault number two: praise to him for remaining in bed while his apartment was on fire, refusing to show undue excitement. Fault number three: praise to him for making his girlfriend stay in bed with him and read from the Sunday comics while the firemen climbed in their window. Fault number four: praise to him for wielding the Pencil of Transubstantiation. Fault number five: praise to him for failing to mention to the students in his living room that he had just stepped over a corpse in his backyard. The Pencil of Transubstantiation. It is made of a fusion of hyper-nanos with atomized neurotransgenesis. Also known as part A and part B. The finger bone connected to the hand bone. Amen.

THE IPOD OF PITHY

Herewith you are kith to the iPod of Pithy. The essence of pithiness. The nit, the grit many have sought to savor. Its slender, stemlike girth in the palm of your hand, the power of which is the grit of the iPod of Pithy. Just having it clipped to your belt makes you kin to a certain flippancy. Whip it out of its sheath, you are with it, hip to the silence at the gist of gist. Your future resembles the ancient past, when withering gods strolled the earth. When Adam slept among the megaliths on par with his trophy wife, Lilith. And that lithe, slithering, fork-tongue Hava, shibboleth, she of the tithing Granny Smith, not yet hither. The iPod of Pithy. You are Picard crouched behind a boulder on the Planet of the Pixilated. You are Pithecanthropus, straddling the width between ape and man. A locksmith with the key to the mysterious monolith, you are pure pithiness, sans the whither, the thither.

The Page of Feathers proffered a feather while the judge pretended to read from the page as he pronounced his sentence. The defense lawyer, having heard it all before, turned off his hearing aid. The defendant, fearing the worst, turned off his pager. There was a little girl sitting in the corner; her name was Page, and her hair was cut in a pageboy. The defendant, who felt guilty even though he had done nothing wrong, felt as if a page had been torn out of his life. He heard that faraway, diminishing sound, which he knew was the new sentence, and already his understanding of it was passé; he would not even catch a glimpse of the new period as it vanished into itself like a collapsing star. Or did it vanish more like the pages of that book he threw into the air-well of a twelve-story hotel where he recalled he had been the only guest, if you did not count the ladies of the night who sat in the lobby turning the pages of a book that explained every dream in the world? Under the topic of Pages, the book said, If you dream of a page being turned by an unseen hand, something small you said a long time ago will one day come back to change everything.

History

The wobbly ceiling fan threatens to decapitate the poetry workshop. They write quickly and nervously. Poetry, the instructor says, is fraught with happenstance and danger. Night in the American South, but the weather, apparently misdirected, has arrived from the Arabian Desert. History enters the room, when Lila, writing about a silk dress, remembers her childless grandfather, tailor to the Shah of Iran. He had laughed at the Shah, there on his knees with his nephews. The Shah, angry, gave him one week to find a second wife who could bear children. Or else. Now Lila sits writing about silk flowing through her grandfather's hands. The ceiling fan shakes like an airplane forcing its way through the wind.

GOTTA HAVE

Cousin Furlow and his dog Keeter and his good-for-nothing pal, Wing Nut. Gotta have a front porch, screened-in, and the screen door. Mandatory poor unfortunate child, tow-headed, albino, with his wrists hanging out of his sleeves. There's got to be crunching of hardtack in his closed mouth to remind us of all Daddy brought home from the war. Gotta go down to the river, it will be dry, except for the mud and dead leaves. Then down to the well we'll go but that's all washing machines, rusty skillets and maybe some unexploded ordnance. Gotta be quiet except for the screen door and what we can't forget Mama said Papa made her do at night. That'll bring back the smell from the whiskey jar beside the bed. We'll have to peer into the blank button eyes of the poor unfortunate child. Gotta see the front yard with dirt swept clean of acorns. And there's Cousin Furlow's limousine held together with Mississippi chrome. Gotta have that shilly-shally white line snaking down two miles of straight road and in the ditch the empty five-gallon paint bucket with the one bullet hole. Gotta have that, for sure—for all we know, that was Mama's way of saying goodbye.

TRIPOD

The barber painted red lines on the sidewalk, across from where he had last seen Sonny. And Grandpa, where was he? Last seen in a trailer made of air that had no windows, no doors. A nearby forest held the evening star hostage. A newspaper was found bound in wire. There were uninvited angels descending rickety ladders in their overalls. It was clear they had been drinking again. Just then, sunset crumbled into ice. A shop that sold rubber bands opened for business. A small dog that had been attacked by an alligator stumbled out of the forest on three legs and joined the boys at the barbershop. They named him Tripod. On Father's Day the barber and Tripod went fishing in the cemetery. Who needs water anyway? Who needs fish? They had three rods, a ball to play with, and a cooler full of beer to sit on.

She was lost inside the rain. But instead of dropping bread-crumbs she put them in her pocket. Each footprint became a tiny lake. Each tiny lake, part of a small stream. Because lightning bugs hide when it rains, Great-Grandfather lost his lightning and could not light her way. There was heat lightning but that was only friction. In another story, Little Sister does not go to school in the rain. She is hiding with Aunt Dot in the woods. Aunt Dot, landlady of the woods. Way, way down, past Birmingham, Alabama. Inside the deafening noise of frogs.

The Drummers

The drummers have returned. They drag their feet in the dust and only beat their drums on occasion. Some drum against their own chests, some drum against their bellies. Some do not drum but think about it sometimes. You could say, what kind of drumming is this anyway? Obviously, not the drumming of the heart; not the famed drum battle between Gene Krupa and Buddy Rich at the Savoy Ballroom in 1953. Not the drumming of a chartreuse butterfly tangled in a spider web. Not the drumming of the milkman's fingers as he recalls how the cream arched up, pressing from beneath the cardboard bottle cap like a seal under ice. But never mind, who cares about the milkman, the nots or the knots or the traveling salesmen or the yo-yo demonstrators? Listen-up! Pay attention! The drummers have returned. They drag their feet in the dust and only beat their drums on occasion.

THE MYSTERIOUS

The Mysterious disappeared one night, just as mysteriously as it had once so long ago mysteriously arrived. Come Back, Mysterious, was a banner pulled by a small plane that later crashed under mysterious circumstances. Now, without The Mysterious, even a word like *circumstances* can seem rather mysterious. *Cir*—a one-ring circus that sets up at dawn and is gone by sunset, leaving no trace. *Cum*—obvious sexual connotations aroused by the mysterious slit in a skirt that opens slightly on a thigh, then closes. *Stances*—those who stand by the sea in their long black overcoats, resembling from a distance the pilings of a pier, a pier whose deck drifted away with the tide, mysteriously.

The mysterious sunglasses stared at the mysterious brassiere. It was hanging from a branch that dangled over the high walls of a cemetery where no one had ever been buried. The mysterious brassiere did not want to be mistaken for a mere bra. Had it not played some part in the duel with sabers in the deserted Chapel of the Holy Mystery? Had it not been used to gather two saving cups of rainwater by two shipwrecked sailors? Meanwhile, The Mysterious itself walked quietly away, leaving the mysterious brassiere and mysterious sunglasses behind. The Mysterious' footprints were faint. But one was slightly deeper than the other, suggesting that it was limping, or had The Mysterious been injured in some way?

Postcard from Pink

You would like Lily. She wears a wig of straight, coal-black hair. She has three wig-mannequins on her dresser. Each is wearing a version of the same wig. There are light bulbs edging her mirror. It is hard to tell how old she is. She must have been a stripper way back when. She wears white pedal-pushers. She has a great body. Her bedroom is done in pink and white. Her Lhasa apso wears a pink collar. I am only here because I am painting her bathroom. Pink. She chews bubblegum but does not make bubbles. I imagine she has a benefactor. I imagine she has a boyfriend. He is a private detective. A former Secret Service man. He was one of the men who were supposed to protect President Kennedy. But the night before the assassination all the Secret Service men partied hard. He was hungover the next day and had his eyes closed behind his dark glasses when the shooting started. Lily ignores me. And why not. I am not a provider or a protector. I am but the applicator of pink. I am writing to you from inside a conch shell. The sound of the paint roller against the wall of the shell is a single note of pink. When I close my eyes I hear the ocean. Sunset, pink sky. Pink froth of waves. Papal pink. Pink smoke. Pink mist. Sniper pink.

The trees here are made of glass, and they are alive. Actually, there is only one tree. It rises out of the lake, a huge scarlet and yellow tower. It feeds on air and plastic cushions that float in the water. When we arrived I was alone. How is that possible? I must have, in our haste to pack, driven off without you. I can picture you standing in the driveway in the predawn light, surprised, or perhaps amused, as the tail-lights of our car recede in the dark. Did you turn and go back to your puzzle? Tomorrow I will try fishing. They say the fish here are also made of glass. The only bait that works on them is tiny, triangular mirrors, each with a number or letter etched into its surface. Figuring out which number or letter is effective at which hour can be a challenge. But locals say that a small #1, trolled on the surface so it creates a V, always works for a few brief but frantic moments, one hour after sunset.

The beach is naked. No sand. No pebbles. No shale. No stones. The waves, as if they were ashamed, roll up to it tentatively, and just before they reach the shore, they turn back. Above, seeming to hang in the wind like mobiles, the skeletons of three gulls. It is said that if you should fall asleep on this beach you'd wake up in your dream and stay there.

A scroll on the Doppler effect written by one Dionysus of Thebes. A book, that when opened, became a kite. It is said that the kite was always the same color as the sky it was flown in. A book that predicted the future. They say it ended with the year 2010. Lost. All lost in the library fire. The tour guide says he stayed up all night reading my poems to his wife. The gum he is chewing does not mask the ouzo on his breath. A former slave, his adopted name is Free Man Ray. There was even a book on the history of the wave that toppled the colossus at Rhodes. Wandering though the ruins without you I wish you were here and that we were strangers. I like the picture on the front, do you? The splayed book, the three roofing nails pinning the pages back, the flames.

Postcard from a Civil War Reenactment

Had breakfast at the Sweet Shop. A placard at the entrance: *Arms and legs where thrown out the second story window. A wagon waited below to receive them.* Last night, I slept at the college. The hallways were lined with empty cots. As was the library, City Hall, the Church of the Redeemer, even the cemetery was lined with cots. I thought there would be formations, marching in step, uniforms, and loud but harmless explosions. I saw an old man wandering through an alley who looked like Walt Whitman. Sometimes he would crouch down close to the ground. He seemed to be speaking to someone. 5:30 a.m., mist low over the fields. I had expected reveille but it was silent. Except for one mockingbird that was imitating the songs of different birds, hoping one would answer, revealing the location of its nest.

A book is a finer pillow than a stone. A drowned book floats face down. A book in a sandstorm constantly changes its mind. Who has not heard of the book, carried over the heart, that stopped a bullet? A watch was in love with a thief, but the thief had many watches. He wore several on each arm. Like most watches, eventually it got sick of dreaming. Nobody cares that the book eats so little to stay alive. Nobody cares about the book of bandages. There is a book looming on the horizon. The book open to the sky is the horizon. What to say about the water bottle? It hardly exists, having already failed as a river. And the rain, tapping its fingers, so impatient, hasn't it already failed as a cloud?

The Chair

Sometimes I wake from a fitful sleep. I have the impression that you have been staring at me while I slept. I reach over to touch you, but you are gone for the day. On your pillow there is a piece of paper that looks like a note. I unfold it and read it. It says: The Chair.

There is a chair at the bottom of Botany Bay. It is embedded in a tub of concrete. Once, the remains of a mobster were tied to the chair. But they have been eaten, disintegrated, floated away in little pieces of bone and belt-buckle and button. Is this the chair you're talking about?

When Pancho Villa, riding with his army, would hear on the radio, El Presidente is seated on his chair, he thought it was a saddle. That is why, in that photograph of him seated, at last, in El Presidente's chair, he looks a bit disappointed. Is this the chair you're talking about?

In the first, exploratory stages of interrogation, unnamed employees of an unnamed government agency will ask you, politely, to please be seated in a chair. Is this the chair you're talking about?

Once, a chair did not get packed into a moving truck. Or maybe it fell out of the moving truck. A beautiful woman found it and would sit on it while she played the cello. Later, the chair was stolen by a homeless man. Because it was an office chair, he was inspired to apply for a job. Because he already had an office chair, he made a favorable impression and was given the job and eventually rose to become Chair of Operations. Is this the chair you're talking about? A great chair is called a throne. The greatest of all chairs is called The Throne of the Third Heaven of the Nations Millennium General Assembly. It was found in a stable. But it is only a facsimile of the throne upon which God is seated, which itself is a larger version of the throne upon which Jesus is seated. Is this the chair you're talking about?

Sometimes when I am at work, sitting, not on a chair, but on an overturned five-gallon bucket, I bite into the sandwich you have made for me. I taste a piece of paper. I extract it from my mouth. I already know what it says, but I read it anyway.

Felsenfeld. He disliked trees because they stayed. He rode a horse across Mali. He could not stop leaving. He could not stop arriving. Felsenfeld, he rode his horse, Chance, across Mali. He kept doves in the bathroom. He could not stop arriving. He blew up his own car. Underneath his overcoat he had a sawed-off shotgun. Was arrested for impersonating a saint. His name like a field. Like the sound of galloping. Traded his wife's dress for a bow. He gave me the bow. For my wedding, he gave me a necklace of tiny skulls he stole from a monastery in Katmandu and a shrunken head from the Amazon. For my wedding, a necklace of tiny skulls. I could not keep it: lost, the bow with its long, serrated fishing arrows. He could not stop leaving or arriving. His name, like water cascading down a long stairway.

THE ALIBI ROOM

A dog is sleeping at the entrance to The Alibi Room. No, you decide as you step over him—he is dead. Perhaps for a few days. He was the stray dog. Now the town will need a new stray dog. Felsenfeld is sitting at the bar. Norris the bartender is lying asleep on the floor. His left foot is twitching. Felsenfeld sits perfectly still. He reminds you of a photo you saw once of a bar in Lebanon after a terrorist attack. An attractive woman in an evening dress with a drink in front of her. One elbow on the bar, a cigarette in her hand. She looked as if she were signaling the bartender. But she was dead. If only the town was not named Lassitude. It could have been called Lassie Town. Or Attitude Town. If only The Alibi Room had not been named The Alibi Room. It could have been called Al's Bar. Or The Alabama. Or The Ali Baba. Felsenfeld steps over Norris and pours me a tall one.

We thought we were in another town so I asked this man who was sitting on the curb, What town is this? He answered, We Thought We Were in Another Town. I thought he was a wise guy and considered smacking him. But then I noticed the sign: WE THOUGHT WE WERE IN ANOTHER TOWN. POPULATION 200.

No one comes here on purpose. No one wants to leave after they have tasted the waffles at the We Thought We Were in Another Town Café. Felsenfeld started walking out of town as if he were balancing on the white line on the road. Every few steps he would stop, and stand there with his arms spread out like a scarecrow. It was his special dance. He called it The Felsenfeld Movement and said that it would catch on someday. He began to add new moves, slow, underwater-like moves.

Confusion

The road into Confusion was downhill and coated with ice. I wondered as we slid, my foot not touching the break, if there was only one stoplight in Confusion, and if that was it at the bottom of the hill, and if it would change from red to green. Felsenfeld scrunched low in his seat, an unlit Pall Mall dangling from his lip, the visor of his cap over his eyes. If I wake up dead, he whispered, I'll kill you. I remember reading in the guidebook that the original name of Confusion was Quandary. As we spun in circles through the intersection I noticed how quiet it was, how slowly we turned, or were we absolutely still, and Confusion was revolving all around us? This seemed like a good time for a little known fact. I said, Did you know that the first toilet seen on television was on *Leave It to Beaver*? Felsenfeld did not answer. He was asleep, an unlit Pall Mall dangling from his lip.

No One

Felsenfeld changed his name to No One. No One climbs a cliff to take a baby eagle for a pet. No One sneaks tiny monkeys past airport security, safely hidden in his overcoat, until they get out in the men's room. No One and his brother are on hands and knees, climbing stalls, chasing little monkeys. His brother says, I see how it is with you now that I have chased monkeys on my hands and knees in the airport men's room. Verily, I could have told him. And if you drive across the desert with No One, he won't let you drive. You might end up chasing the car, as it rolls on its own toward a crater that has become a dry lake bed. You might end up out of gas next to a wooden, hand-lettered sign: ALKALI FLATS—100 MILES FROM NOWHERE, 2 FEET FROM HELL. No One sets his car on fire. Dining out with friends, he shows off his skill at eating small sections off the rim of his wine glass. It was then we realized that one day No One would tire of this world. But No One had already disappeared. It was after I said, I'll call you tomorrow. Tomorrow came many years later. But by then he had changed his name to the less formal Nobody.

Arriving at last in Vowelville we were greeted by the Vole. At least he said that was his name. But Felsenfeld said to me later when we were at the Vowelville Motel, where we were the only guests, That man is not the Vole, the Mole or even the Bole. It was all the same to me. That night I was startled out of sleep by a startling sound. It was unsettling and indescribable, like restless leg syndrome. What was it? Felsenfeld was no help—he just slept on. But something had changed in the world. Something, perhaps in the atmosphere, had been rent, and would never be the same. Many years later, after I learned that Felsenfeld had died, I read about the Great Vowel Shift. Swineherds who said *potato* now said *potahto*. Churlish marauders would tilt their chins up and say *rahther*, rather than *rather*. Now I know what Felsenfeld had known all along. Something that night had changed and would never be the same.

MISSING ONE

You lay the paint chip labeled Missing One on the table. You pick up Blueberry and Sweet-Talk. But face it, Missing One suits you. You've always been Missing One. The one no one remembers in the photograph. The almost gray of what you wished you had said but did not. Some say Missing One is just slightly tinted white. That there are many like it. That there is even a Missing Two, and a Missing Three. But Manuel, the house painter, given to superstition, never speaks its name, just referring to it by its number, 001. He has learned to ignore the elastic holes he sees opening and closing in the air whenever he pries open a gallon of Missing One. He knows better than to believe what his senses tell him: no matter how appealing, Missing One does not really smell like banana milkshake. He wonders if Missing One has a sound? Would it be like the coin dropped into the abandoned mine shaft at Los Pozos, Mexico? A deep, deep hole inside a cave. No guard railing, no ladder. You toss a peso into the darkness and wait. And wait.

H is a piece of ladder. Or a short kid afraid he won't grow. He gets his friends to pull on his arms and legs. There is a popping sound. It seems to him that after that, he begins to grow. The E is another piece of broken ladder. 1 is a stick. Never very many toys, but plenty of sticks. A rifle, a bow, a sword, a cane if he is wounded in the war. 7 rides his bike, coasting downhill with his feet off the pedals—Look at me, he yells, One hand! Wakes up in a hospital. His buddies, a 5, a 6 and a 3, all standing around the bed. Who are they? He does not recall their names. The smartass kid with his cap on backwards. The chubby one. The boy with the small waist and curves who looks like a girl. Back home, in his room, he plays detective. He can poke a skeleton key out of a keyhole; it falls on the newspaper he has placed under the door. Someone is dialing. He listens to the clicks of the dial, counting. H is four clicks. E is three. One click. Seven clicks. Night comes striding, dark, starless, cold. And he remembers the cry of the peacocks.

The Three

The bear did not return as he had promised. Parachutes bloomed and drifted silently into the darkness of that moment just before sleep, nodding as if in agreement.

It was then that the boy remembered there were three things he was supposed to remember. Did one go this way, or was it that way?

Maybe one got lost like the soldiers returning from the war and entering the wrong houses. But the houses were almost like their own houses. They recalled towers in flames, torn banners dangling from minarets.

But still, the bear did not return. Sometimes the boy could sense him in the rustle of leaves at the edge of the forest. He imagined him standing against a tree in a clearing, waiting for silence, for attention, as if he were about to tell a story.

The bear did not return as he had promised. So the child never left the cottage. Never Left the Cottage became his name— that's what the hunters called him. Never spoke, never answered, although sometimes he did hop about the room like a sparrow on the grass, a tiny sparrow about to take flight.

Someday he would remember and tell them about The Three: three ways at the crossroads, three words to say or not to say, or maybe which three stars to follow.

They noticed that when light came into the room, not just daylight, but a beam with spirals of dust suspended in it like a diagram, the child welcomed it like an old friend, and moved his lips, silently.

The bear did not return as he had promised. So the child never left the cottage. The tree refused to grow.

Grandma Nana decided to cut it down. She swung her axe into its bark and it bled. She decided to leave the tree alone.

The boy dreamt that he was the only one who knew the answer to the riddle: The bear, the cottage, the tree. Or was it the stars, the crossroads, the words? He set off to find where everyone had gone. When he looked back, it seemed the tree was much taller.

83

Eighty-three words leap from their horses. Eighty-three words all lie down, each bearing a sign on their chest. One forgot his hat, one forgot a feather. Not words, but Little Big Horn battle re-enactors at a sushi restaurant. No wonder they were confused. How can a horn be little and big at the same time? A man sitting beside me turned to face me. Can you lower your voice, he said. Surprise, it was my deceased father dressed up as Crazy Horse, that dandy.

There are times a man has to choose between a feather and a bullet; my father told me this. I've made a list of all the things he told me that were important, and this is first. Strange as it seems, there are eighty-three things on the list and he died on his eighty-third birthday, eighty-three days after my mother passed. There's no explanation for this. And yesterday I was dismayed to discover my car is parked eighty-three steps from my front door. In numerology eighty-three stands for eternity and a half.

They say Crazy Horse was late for the battle of Little Big Horn because he kept changing his outfits. Finally he had it right, his cream buckskins with the red tassels. At the end of each tassel, a crow feather. His braves, who had been waiting impatiently, were relieved to see him come out of his tent. At that very moment in eternity, my father came out of the bathroom of the sushi restaurant.

When Crazy Horse was murdered, eighty-three braves, in war colors with long headdresses of eagle feathers, danced around his body. The history of eighty-three is written on the back of a sushi menu in downtown Los Angeles and memorized in Japanese by each sushi chef. That's what I love about eighty-three—the color, the history. The only other number with a comparable story is one hundred and eleven, yes, one hundred and eleven. But there's so much heartbreak there it makes me sob to tell.

It's Like

It's like the phone rings but the person on the other end has forgotten how to speak. It's like trying to hold on to clumps of dollar weed, but a giant hand is shaking you off. Or do you fall into space, getting smaller and smaller, and when you drift over the moon you look down and see three dead Russian cosmonauts lying on their backs as if they were sleeping? Is that what's bothering you, Bunkie? It's like you're in bed looking at the clock, which has become a red patch pasted on the ceiling. And the alarm goes off and it's 3 a.m., it's *Stars and Stripes Forever* and a deep voice shouting, Buck up! Get a grip! Isn't this, you think, when most people die? And you gasp, your throat sucking in air with a series of snorts. Aren't you sorry now that you said breathing was overrated?

LIKE TWO PEOPLE

I fell into bed like a cascade of fiberglass filters or more like a bowl of cold oatmeal. Tossing and turning was like pulling weeds in warm rain, until my wife said, Go read a book, one that calls to you like a phone ringing in an abandoned airport. Then I slept as if I had never existed and jumped out of bed like a harlequin astride a palomino. I shimmied sideways in the shower like a car skidding across five lanes of rush-hour traffic. Then I wrote a poem that tried to draw Rodin's *Balzac* from memory. My wife came home for lunch and handed me a note like a blind bank robber. It said, Please mow the lawn like a stevedore braving the gauntlet of challenge and I will love you like an angel that has forgotten the sky. I made her an omelet but she was afraid to touch it, as if it were a sleepwalker standing on a construction girder twelve stories high. I lay down to nap on the couch, forgetting that I had left my baseball cap on. It remained on my head while I slept like a cat in a banana tree. My dreams were deep and uncontrollable, as if I were like two people, twins, both accountants, both in love with each other's spouse, also twins.

I got out of bed like a decomposing century of death. I had been in a dream in which we were together like a steel daisy and a rose made of razor wire. Then I took a shower, all the while thinking of you, and my thoughts were a robin frozen on your lawn or maybe a snowman in a blizzard. So I drove to work, which is actually next door to the bedroom. My office reminded me of a blood-soaked hairdresser—at least that's what I thought, until I wrote a poem that hit me on the head like a book falling out of the sky. Later I rode my bike through a park that was like a hot iron I thought was unplugged. All the bare trees made me think of Vlad the Impaler, but the birds were chirping like explosions in reverse. Or was it bald trees, or bards, or tresses instead of trees? Bike—poem—thoughts of you—all in all, a successful day. Time for a nap, and I slept like a duck in a phone booth. Again, I dreamt of you, picking up where we had left off. You and I together just like . . . like shards of falling glass. Except that I was just like two people, someone named You and a person named I. Once again my brain waited for me to wake like the basket waiting beneath the guillotine. But it was too late; already I had begun interviewing myself. I was also a panel on *Keeping the Faith*. I was the audience too—sometimes bored and skeptical of my answers, sometimes amused, but cautiously so, like a lion tamer with narcolepsy.

Talk about shadows had overshadowed the afternoon. Then a tropical evening with light rain was delivered by mistake and we felt giddy. As if we were on vacation, and about to meet someone interesting. Like ominous music, the shadow of the earth dissected a crater on the moon. As if the waiter moving so inconspicuously among us was a spy. In one corner, poets from Los Angeles were discussing traffic. But you, you were like the rain, not caring if you disappeared into the ocean. Oh well, I thought, as I brushed a tiny bit of cake from your cheek and placed it on my tongue, even a shadow can cast a shadow. There is a lost shoe on the bottom of the ocean. The shoe is right next to a claw-foot bathtub. In some poems the shoe and the bathtub would not speak to each other. The poets from Los Angeles were discussing secret shortcuts. The shoe thought it had a lot in common with the bathtub, both being hollow, singular, and somewhat out of place. How lucky we were to step out into the evening that had been delivered to us, even if it was a mistake, to let the frothy chill of surf stun us into feeling alive. We stood knee-deep in the ocean and raised our empty glasses to the rain.

A man could not decide if his belt was too tight or too loose. Sometimes, in bed, he could not decide if he was hot or cold. He put on his long-johns and socks. He took them off and lay under the blankets, a thin layer of cold perspiration coating his skin. On the treadmill, he did not know if he was walking forward or backward. It was the same when he was stopped in traffic and the cars started to move and his car seemed to be drifting backward and he would slam on the breaks. There was this place he remembered that bothered him because it did not exist except in his memory. He had dreamt about it, perhaps several times, or he had dreamt once that he had dreamt about it several times. A run-down building in the Mission district of San Francisco, divided into cheap apartments. The walls were painted white, the doors red. Mildew, doors slamming, worn-out carpet. Maybe it was a place that he had forgotten and then dreamt about. He thought, if I woke up in the dark and did not know where I was, I could spit to see if I was upside down or right side up. He thought, if I were a spider blown across a mirror on a front lawn I would think that I was sliding against the sky.

Get up off that couch. Flap your arms. Do The Chicken Dance. Do The Chicket. Do *El Pollo Loco*. Go out into the yard where the bamboo grove leans on its side, and the wind, spinning in a circle, goes clack-a-clack-a-clack. Pretend you're dodging bullets in slow motion. Now it's time to become a famous painter you admire, for you have stepped into a painting of the backyard; each blade of grass stiff with intention, each blade of grass awaiting further instructions. Now jump rope and flap your wings. Say, Miss Mary Mack Mack, won't pay you back back back. Jump like you're doing easy-overs with your best pal, Ernie. Okay, go back inside. Stand in the middle of the room, in front of the television. I know, it's broken, but turn it on so you can hear it sizzle, swish, and hiss. Now make like you're Anthony Quinn in *La Strada*. After a year of not even thinking about her, you hear that Gelsomina, little clown who played the snare drum, who loved you so, whom you mistreated, is dead. You're at the beach. Kneel in the sand; beat the cold water with your big wings. Stand and stumble around in your chicken feet and cry, cry like you've never cried before.

Blondes are disappearing from the world. Just yesterday, one sat cross-legged on my desk looking all blonde and dangerous. She was staring at her nails, which were painted deep blue. She seemed just about to speak when she disappeared, leaving her fox stole behind, its little glass eyes staring up at me.

My red-headed wife confesses she's a blonde. And her name is not really Katherine, but Linda. That's OK, I never knew my first wife's real name until I was walking out the door with my golf clubs slung over my shoulder, while the cabdriver, claiming the right of salvage, gathered my neckties from the front lawn.

In a country where there are no blondes, even fake blondes can make big trouble. My wife, looking over my shoulder as I write this, says, You've never had a lawn, you don't golf, and you don't even know how to tie a necktie. Go color your roots, I say, the blonde is showing through.

The government of Sweden has convened an emergency session. Icelandic police are gathering up Icelandic blondes and taking them to an undisclosed location. Back at the office I lean back in my chair. I wonder why it's only blonde women who are disappearing. I open up the newspaper: no more blondes in Minnesota.

I look through the files in my computer. Blondes are disappearing from my poems: the one who had tried to poison me with developer fluid; the one I ran over with a motorcycle; the one who was last seen in the Amazon jungle smearing mud on her body that contained flecks of gold; the one who tempted me to follow her out into the rain when I was in bed with the flu.

Just then my wife, roots freshly dyed copper-red, strides into my office. She sits on my desk as if she owns the place. Stares at her cobalt nails.

They met at the Rory Calhoun Film Festival. She was wearing a black cowboy hat just like Rory Calhoun wore in *The Rider*. He sported a fedora, a replica of the one that Rory Calhoun wore in *Hijack*. Her first words to him were, You look like a holy barbarian. Ah yes, he said, you refer to *The Beatniks*, Rory Calhoun's least-known picture, in which he was unshaven, wore a sweatshirt and played bongos in a dive where Beatniks read poetry; but actually, he was a detective on the hunt for a missing heiress. Impressed by his knowledge, she knew in that moment that she wanted to die with him in a black Studebaker that plunged over a cliff, tumbled down a hillside and exploded, just like Rory Calhoun and Veronica Lake in *Diamonds to Dust*. Veronica Lake, that's who she reminded him of. The blonde hair flowing, covering one side of her face, revealing, concealing. They would never know that they had been in the same kindergarten, that they had been born on the same day in the same hospital, that they were twins, separated at birth, stolen by baby traffickers. They would never know that even before they were born they were Rory Calhoun fans, as their mother sat alone in the dark watching Rory Calhoun in *Dark Angel*, while they lay side by side in her womb, each of them attempting to devour the other.

DOLLAR THEATER

Sometimes I feel like Heidi coming home to her village. All along the valley there are cries, Heidi is coming home, Heidi is coming home, church bells are ringing, even the brook is ringing. The bag lady stops rustling through her bag. The man under the huge overcoat stops snoring. Sometimes I feel like Bogart. Sitting with my drink, an Egyptian cigarette dangling from my lips. I'm cursing my luck at seeing you again. It's like that dream where you walk into the room and I wake up. Then I fall asleep and you're putting the flowers you brought into a vase, then I wake up. Sometimes I feel like Frankenstein. I'm staring at my strange hand, my strange leg, I'm all made up of different people and I'm wondering if they ever knew each other.

Hackers can turn your computer into a bomb. They can be in Mumbai and you can be in Bozeman, Montana. It is your first day at your new job. You type the ampersand and boom—you're spattered all over the office. Maybe the last thought you have is Mama Told Me Not to Come. Hackers can stare into your house through the computer screen. They can hypnotize you with the cursor, planting a posthypnotic suggestion that when you hear the song "My Sharona" you'll bounce your chin repeatedly against your chest. Hackers can make you say It's Just My Imagination Running Away With Me. Hackers can make your spirit abandon your body as if you were dead. Hackers can make you walk like Wayne Newton with your blank, wide eyes seeing nothing. Hackers can make you dance The Hustle like a cartoon with only your arms and legs moving. Dogs will bark at you from deep inside your computer screen. Hackers can make you think the dogs are singing Oh Daddy, Don't Walk Away So Fast.

TAKE

Take that pampas grass we offered in honor of the Empress and take the Empress too. I prefer the tower struck by lightning. What shall we do with your father, pounding the door while we make love on the carpet? Thus the convoy of grocery carts filled with our belongings at midnight when he would no longer pay the rent. Here is a list of things I wish I had not given to the Salvation Army: my black leather jacket with zippers on the sleeves. The silver ring embossed with crescent moons. My orange, yellow, green, blue, red, and silver disco shirt. Take the ghosts with you. Or at least, tell them to quit standing around my bed like skeleton surgeons over a comatose patient. Why did you carry those orange peels from apartment to apartment? I'll go wait for you in the park at that open field. It was there that I last saw my Australian boomerang diminish.

and fell into his own body. He fell for a long time. He had expected to see pulsing veins and red flesh, but the walls of his body were more like an elevator shaft. Objects were embedded against the walls. A display of some kind. As if the objects, pliers, broken cups, an office chair, had fallen into his body and become stuck to the walls. What was he, public art? An abandoned well? There was a favorite shirt that he lost many years ago. He would have reached for it but it would no longer fit him anyway. Falling through his own body, the man thought that he should brace himself to hit bottom. He braced himself. He managed to curl himself into a ball. But that set him spinning, fast, and the objects in the wall became a blur. He wanted to see the objects flash by, so he unrolled himself and continued to fall. Oh, and there was something shiny in the wall. Maybe it was the ring he had always thought was stolen by his brother-in-law. The silver one with the crescent moons carved into it. How he loved that ring. He began to wonder as he was falling through his own body, what else would he see embedded in the walls? He felt something pleasant, a hopeful anticipation. It was as if he had forgotten that he was falling. No—more like he enjoyed falling through his own body.

The moon left a note on the table. Now you can't find it. At least, that is what Nobody says. You call him Nobody because he has no body. Maybe he stole the note. It was the tide that pulled the moon into its tangle. Or was it tango? Whatever it was, the tide was to blame. That's why the hair on my forearm was frightened. It was the rabbit's sky. A murderer's knife left in the cold. A tired girlfriend defeated all hope for the immediate future. You're bamboozled with chilled tangelos right on cue. Just another memorial; deserted battlefield of memory. Ask not how the bells flap and clap without you. No bong for Mr. Bong. No applause. Please. Keep your hands clenched in your pockets like hand grenades.

There was a man who slept on his back in the sand with his arms raised to the sky. My arms are the twin towers, he thought, attempting to resist a dream. My feet are Babylon. My stomach is where snipers hide. There was a man who came to rescue the people. Oh really, said the people. Let us greet you with arms full of flowers. With arms. There was a man who lived in a tower, most disturbed by bees, by corrosive mold and dusty rust. By loving couples, strangers exchanging portraits in the dark, immune to peeling paint, curtains sailing about in the wind mimicking fog. We are embedded in the fog, said one stranger to another. It was dawn over Baghdad, but neither stranger believed in light.

THE ABANDONING

People stroll past in groups of three or fours. Some in couples. All silent, all with their arms crossed against their chests. Sunlight flashes from their silver-painted fingernails. Who would have thought that light could absorb so much of The Abandoning? Now these same people are walking back in the opposite direction. Some carry a frond of pampas grass held aloft like a green and white crowbar to pry against an edge of The Abandoning. Just when did The Abandoning happen? Were there many Abandonings, or just one? No one knows, but downtown there is a stepladder embedded in concrete, some say it is the letter A, but others say it is a memorial to The Abandoning.

THE DURATION

Nothing much happened during The Duration. But a child did say the word duration until its meaning disappeared. Cream puffs reigned supreme. Baked Alaska was big during The Duration. We thought it would be a kind of interlude but, technically, it could have been forever. Snowdrifts were also popular. Something white, like laundry, hovered over the land. In a darkened circus tent, a hobo clown tried to sweep a circle of light into a dustpan. It was The Duration. The way it eluded the broom. The way he could never quite sweep it up as it contracted, becoming smaller and smaller, as the dark grew larger.

THE WAITING

I have been waiting for you so long. I have made you a cairn of stone. The night speaks to the dish that listens to the sky. It speaks in a language only the night understands. Nothing is on the ground to block your way. No vegetation, no dirt, nothing alive, only stone. And if you were to come and walk with me we would find nothing on the flat ground except an occasional small meteorite. The fog hums to the silence in a language only the fog understands. I thought I heard your voice last night. I thought you put your mouth to my ear. Your breath was as cold as stone. You said, The fog is on fire.

The Aftermath arrived uninvited, without retinue, or precedent. Gray sunlight was gradually suspended. Stars formed in cliques, giggling, carrying on. Cosmic rays continued to probe unabated, as The Aftermath remained, uninvited. Several numbers piled on the couch, but added up to nothing. Blame The Aftermath. Single-windowed souls were admitted, some bringing gifts of pomade. Tiny sandwiches were served, each of related interest. Low-grade voluptuousness eventually passed into sleep. The Aftermath sat in a corner. No one spoke to it. The nerve.

THE PANTS DANCE

A brown pair of pants walking across the room. Is this the same pair of pants a spirit held up to my mother when she asked what sex I would be? My pants cower under the bed, cowardly pants. My pants swing on the clothesline. My pants follow me into the Voodoo Lounge. Stupid pants, I thought I told you to wait in the truck. You can dance with your pants. It's called The Pants Dance. It's a dance for old men. You are permitted to dance sitting in your chair waving your pants around your head.

ACKNOWLEDGMENTS

Grateful acknowledgment is made to the editors of the following print and online journals, in which these poems appeared, sometimes in slightly different form or with different titles:

2River: "The Aftermath," "The Duration," "Nightstand";
13 Miles from Cleveland: "Postcard from Pink";
42 Opus: "Postcard from a Nude Beach," "Undecided";
Big City Lit: "Little Known Fact Number Two"; "Subservient Chicken";
Big Toe Review: "Dollar Theater," "Hemlock 1-7563," "Page," "October," "The Pencil of Transubstantiation," "The Poker-Playing Dog Poetry Workshop";
Cease, Cows: "The History of White Anklets," "Helen's Birthday," "Vowelville";
CEliA's Round Trip: "The Alibi Room," "Missing One";
Connotation Press: "The Duration";
Dirty Napkin: "Little Known Fact Number One," "No One";
In Posse Review: "The Pants Dance";
Jelly Bucket: "Little Known Fact Number Three," "My Angry Mob," "November First," "The Religious Brain," "The Unstucks at the Gates of the Desert Folly Garden";
Mead: "The History of the Minstrel Show," "A Portrait of My Childhood Painted by Goya," "The Rory Calhoun Film Festival";
Mental Shoes: "November First," "Upraised Arms";
Mid-American Review: "Former Lovers" "The Expert";
Other Voices International Project, Volume 43: "His Last Night," "Postcard from Pink";
Poemeleon: "The Case of the Disappearing Blondes," "Felsenfeld," "The Felsenfeld Movement," "Confusion";
Praxilla: "The iPod of Pithy," "Sappho," *Tristes Tropiques*";
Qarrtsiluni: "83," "The Three";
Rattle: "Just Like Two People";

Re:Union: "His Last Night";
Rhino: "The Poker-Playing Dog Poetry Workshop";
Shadowbox: "Footsteps," "Matchbook," "Tanglewood";
Spillway: "The Abandoning," "Day at the Beach, 1958";
Tumbir: "Just Like Two People";
Tupelo Press Fragments from Sappho: "Sappho";
Twelve Stories: "The Chair";
Willows Wept Review: "The Three."

"Postcard from Lake Manzanita" and "The Poetry Lesson" appear in *Bear Flag Republic: Prose Poems and Poetics from California*, ed. Christopher Buckley and Gary Young (Greenhouse Review Press/ Alcatraz Editions, 2008).

"Postcard from a Civil War Reenactment" appears in *Found Anew: New Writing Inspired by the South Caroliniana Library Digital Collections*, ed. by Ray McManus and R. Mac Jones (University of South Carolina Press, 2014).

Some of these poems appeared in the chapbook, *Chickenhead*, Foothills Publishing (Kanona, NY, 2009).

"The Poetry Lesson" is for Charles Harper Webb.

"Hemlock-1-7563" is for Ernesto "Tito" Alaniz.

"83" was written with Rick Bursky.

The "Felsenfled" poems are in memory of Thomas Nash Glynn.

This book is dedicated to Katherine.

Richard Garcia is the author of five books of poetry: *The Flying Garcias* (University of Pittsburgh Press, 1991); *Rancho Notorious* (BOA Editions, 2001); *The Persistence of Objects* (BOA Editions, 2006); *Chickenhead*, a chapbook of prose poems (Foothills Publishing, 2009); and *The Other Odyssey* (Dream Horse Press, 2014). He is also the author of *My Aunt Otilia's Spirits*, a bilingual children's book (Children's Book Press,1978). Garcia's poems appear widely in such journals as *The Antioch Review*, *The Colorado Review*, and *The Georgia Review*, and in several anthologies, including *The Best American Poetry 2005*, *Touching the Fire*, *Seriously Funny*, and *The Best of the Prose Poem*. His awards and accolades include a fellowship from the National Endowment for the Arts, the Pushcart Prize, the Cohen Award from *Ploughshares*, the *Georgetown Review* Poetry Prize, and the *American Poetry Journal* Book Prize. From 1991 to 2002, he was a Poet-in-Residence at Children's Hospital in Los Angeles, California, where he conducted poetry and art workshops for hospitalized children. Garcia teaches creative writing in the Antioch University Low-Residency MFA program. He currently lives on James Island, South Carolina, with his wife and their dogs Sully and Max.

BOA Editions, Ltd. American Poets Continuum Series

Colophon

BOA Editions, Ltd., a not-for-profit publisher of poetry and other literary works, fosters readership and appreciation of contemporary literature. By identifying, cultivating, and publishing both new and established poets and selecting authors of unique literary talent, BOA brings high-quality literature to the public. Support for this effort comes from the sale of its publications, grant funding, and private donations.

❖

The publication of this book is made possible, in part,
by the special support of the following individuals:

Anonymous x 4
Nin Andrews
Armbruster Family Foundation
Bernadette Catalana, *in memory of Irving Pheterson*
Robert L. Giron
Suzanne Gouvernet
Michael Hall
Sandi Henschel, *in honor of her daughter Lisa Richele Piccione*
Willy & Bob Hursh
Barbara & John Lovenheim
Peter & Phyllis Makuck
Chandra V. McKenzie
Boo Poulin
Deborah Ronnen & Sherman Levey
Steven O. Russell & Phyllis Rifkin-Russell
Joe Turri, *in memory of Debra Audet*
Jillian Weise
Patricia & Michael Wilder

/6⁰⁰

RECEIVED OCT 5 - 2017

DISCARD